SandCastle™

Mini Animal Marvels

# Miniature
# Primates

A Division of ABDO

**ABDO**
Publishing Company

**Alex Kuskowski**     Consulting Editor, Diane Craig, M.A./Reading Specialist

# visit us at www.abdopublishing.com

Printed in the United States of America, North Mankato, Minnesota
102013
012014

 PRINTED ON RECYCLED PAPER

Editor: Liz Salzmann
Content Developer: Alex Kuskowski
Cover and Interior Design and Production: Mighty Media, Inc.
Photo Credits: Shutterstock, iStockphoto

**Library of Congress Cataloging-in-Publication Data**

Kuskowski, Alex.
  Miniature primates / Alex Kuskowski.
      pages cm. -- (Mini animal marvels)
  ISBN 978-1-62403-068-0
1. Primates--Juvenile literature. 2. Primates--Size--Juvenile literature. I. Title.
  QL737.P96.K87 2014
  599.8--dc23
                              2013022907

## SandCastle™ Level: Transitional

SandCastle™ books are created by a team of professional educators, reading specialists, and content developers around five essential components—phonemic awareness, phonics, vocabulary, text comprehension, and fluency—to assist young readers as they develop reading skills and strategies and increase their general knowledge. All books are written, reviewed, and leveled for guided reading, early reading intervention, and Accelerated Reader® programs for use in shared, guided, and independent reading and writing activities to support a balanced approach to literacy instruction. The SandCastle™ series has four levels that correspond to early literacy development. The levels are provided to help teachers and parents select appropriate books for young readers.

| Emerging Readers (no flags) | Beginning Readers (1 flag) | Transitional Readers (2 flags) | Fluent Readers (3 flags) |

# Table of Contents

# Miniature Primates

Miniature **primates** are very small primates. **Apes**, monkeys, and lemurs are primates.

# Philippine Tarsier

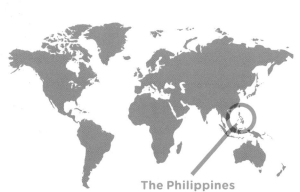

The Philippines

The Philippine tarsier
is a small **primate**.
It jumps from tree
to tree.

6 feet
(1.8 m)

It is 6 inches
(15.2 cm) long.

6 inches
(15.2 cm)

Philippine tarsiers come out at night. They see with their big eyes. They hunt for small bugs.

# Pygmy Marmoset

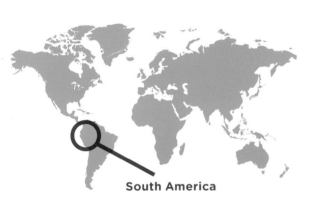

South America

The pygmy marmoset is the smallest monkey. It lives in the rain forest.

6 feet
(1.8 m)

It is 5 inches
(12.7 cm) long.

5 inches
(12.7 cm)

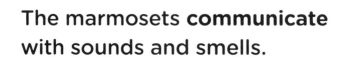

The marmosets **communicate** with sounds and smells.

Pygmy marmosets live in groups. Most are born **twins**.

# Mouse Lemur

Madagascar

The mouse lemur is a very small **primate**. It lives high up in the trees.

6 feet
(1.8 m)

It is 5 inches
(12.7 cm) long.

5 inches
(12.7 cm)

Mouse lemurs hide during the day. They come out to eat at night.

# Emperor Tamarin

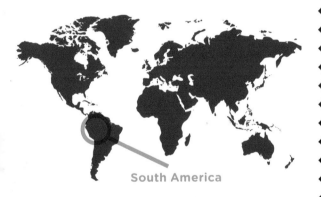

South America

The emperor tamarin is a very small monkey. It eats plants and tiny bugs.

6 feet
(1.8 m)

It is 10 inches
(25.4 cm) long.

10 inches
(25.4 cm)

Emperor tamarins have very long tails. Their tails are brown.

The emperor tamarin has a **mustache**. It is very long.

# Did You Know?

 Philippine tarsiers cannot move their eyes.

 Pygmy marmosets live 12 years.

 One kind of mouse lemur is the smallest **primate**.

 Emperor tamarins live in groups.

# Primate Quiz

1 Philippine tarsiers only eat plants.

2 Philippine tarsiers come out at night.

3 Most pygmy marmosets are born **twins**.

4 Mouse lemurs eat during the day.

5 The emperor tamarin has a brown tail.

Answers: 1. False 2. True 3. True 4. False 5. True

# Glossary

**ape** – a large animal related to humans and monkeys. Chimpanzees and gorillas are apes.

**communicate** – to share ideas, information, or feelings.

**mustache** – the hair that grows on the upper lip.

**primate** – a mammal with developed hands and feet, a large brain, and a short nose, such as a human, ape, or monkey.

**twin** – one of two babies born to the same mother at the same birth.